A GLOBAL VIEW ON AMAZON FBA

AMAZON FBA SECRETS REVEALED

FINALLY, A STEP BY STEP GUIDE TO FBA SUCCESS

By Jose Joseph

Table of Contents

Introduction

Before we go into anything concerning Amazon FBA and how easy it is to get something out of the platform, I would like to address some things. The first of them is the fact that nothing good comes easy. The process is simple but by no means easy. This book is simple to understand. It is not written in massively fluffy and intricate words that makes the reader snore and aims to confuse. The aim of this book is to deliver the message in such a way that a 10-year-old would be able to understand and put the knowledge into practice.

This is the mentality I want you to have about the process we are embarking on. I also want you to know that even though we are about to pave the way for you in terms of information, you will have your own set of challenges and obstacles because if we all had the same story to tell, then it would be more of a movie than a phase. Irrespective of what you are going to pass through, I want you to promise yourself you will make the best of what is right in front of you. If you know you are going to quit, then you might as well do it right away rather than later. However, if you are ready to move with me, then we have a lot of work to do – I relay the information in terms of my experiences, and it is up to you to put it to work – and you have to make sure you take action because that is the only thing that will yield results; action.

There are millions and millions of people who know everything there is to know about Amazon FBA and how they can make something out of it, but then they procrastinate, and for some others, they face the smallest challenges, and they chicken out. This cannot be you. You must not allow this to be the case with you, and as I said earlier, if you are not ready to put in time, you might as well not commit the crime – just stop and do something else, for instance, continue watching movies.

Why am I so harsh with my statements from the very beginning? Because I have been there. I had a lot of information, and yet I just chewed popcorn with the information, and tomorrow never stopped because I was ready to put it off till the next day. Days went by, weeks, months, and years and you sit down at some point and ask yourself what have I done this year, and all you can look at are your uploads on Twitter and Instagram. Yes, we thank God for life, but are you making the most of it? You answer this.

In this book, "Amazon FBA secrets revealed," we are not for any reason:

- Going to embrace any complexities just to add to the number of pages in this book.
- Going to make any false promises that you are guaranteed to make money because that is a lie – Amazon and the information here are the constants, and you are the variable.
- It's going to feed you with false figures to make you excited only for you to dash your foot upon a stone when you find out that it's all a lie.

All we are going to do is get you on the right track with easy to understand information and the rest is up to you. No matter how lazy people are today, taking social media as a standard of life rather than embracing the reality that the time to make the most of your life is here, I believe in you. I believe that you understand what lies ahead because in all honesty, buying this book is the first step towards making a profitable living out of the Amazon FBA program and who knows what's to come because believe me, once you can see it, work with it and run with it, then there is a lot to achieve. Let's go make that money.

Chapter 1

Overview of Amazon FBA

Amazon FBA is now just about the most popular and genuine way to generate income online. In reality, more than two million folks are selling on Amazon anywhere. Any person could list a product on the Amazon market, whether it is an item you have bought and want to sell, made yourself, or just something you don't need. In case you sign up for the FBA plan, you can automate order fulfillment by using Amazon's innovative delivery and fulfillment services and generate additional product sales from Amazon's Prime customers.

About 50% of most sales on Amazon originate from third-party sellers, and outside of the leading 10,000 sellers, 67% of them apply FBA – this should tell you something here. Before going any further, let's discuss and understand Amazon FBA.

What is Amazon FBA?

FBA stands for Fulfillment by Amazon. What that amounts to is: you source and market it, Amazon ships it.

Let's look at how this works:

1. You send out the products to Amazon.
2. They keep them in the warehouses.
3. When a person orders one of the products, Amazon packs, picks, ships, and also monitors the purchase.
4. They additionally handle refunds and returns.

Each one of these does come at a cost. Amazon charges both storage costs and also fulfillment fees. Nevertheless, those charges include Amazon's exceptional 24/7 customer service, the expense of shipping items to customers, and access to among the biggest & most advanced fulfillment networks on the planet.

Why Amazon FBA Matters

Amazon has over 300 million active buyers, with ninety million Prime members

in the U.S. alone. Brands out there, especially to Prime buyers, are the ones that use FBA. Plus, Prime customers invest much more money with Amazon. The typical buyer usually spends $800 each year on Amazon, while Prime users spend about $1,400 each year. This implies that if you make use of Amazon FBA you are thus far more noticeable to Prime customers; which can lead to earning more cash.

How Amazon FBA Works

Amazon handles all of the work for you within FBA, therefore how it operates is easy.

i.   **Send the products to Amazon**

Amazon has more than 175 operating fulfillment centers across the globe with over 150 million square feet of warehouse storage space. You let them know what items you are bringing in, and they let you know what warehouses to deliver the products to.

ii.   **Amazon then sort and store the products**

Once Amazon gets the products, they will sort and also put them to the inventory. Your items are then stored properly in the warehouses. On the chance that something gets destroyed in the factory, Amazon is going to reimburse you.

iii.   **A person purchases the product.**

Amazon manages the whole transaction for you. They accept payment, and they upgrade your listing automatically.

iv.   Amazon ships the product

One of Amazon's warehouse workers grabs the product from storage space, packs it right into a box and ships it to the buyer.

v.   Amazon manages customer service – well, a great deal of it

After the buyer gets the product, Amazon follows through to ensure they are pleased with the shipment. Additionally, they deal with some questions or returns from the client. As for any feedback, you get it with your item listing; it is up to you to answer and also do something about it. Good reviews mean more business for you as the seller.

vi.   You get paid

Every two weeks, Amazon totals up all the sales, deducts the seller fees, and deposits your profits right into your bank account. That is as simple as it gets! Sound pretty simple? You'll find a couple of things you have to accomplish to ensure you are successful, and we are going to be taking a look at some of this in this book as we move on.

What You are in Charge of When Using Amazon FBA

It looks like Amazon has got everything covered, and for the most part, you are right; however, there are some things you have to do, which is what we are going to be talking about in this section.

Here is what you are accountable for:

1. Selecting what items to sell on Amazon

You can promote almost anything you want, but if you want to stay away from high storage costs, be sure you select products that will sell fast and are smaller in size. You can check out the difference in FBA fees for larger and smaller items. There are also a wide variety of tools available in the market which are aimed at gearing you up for success when considering the selection of items to source and sell.

Keeping the inventory in stock

You will have to check out the inventory levels on Amazon frequently to ensure your goods remain in stock. This is easy to track on the Amazon seller central accounts page.

2. Marketing and advertising the products

When you are promoting highly ranked brand products, you might not need to spend too much time or money marketing your products. But in case you are marketing your very own customized solutions, you will have to make people discover them. You will find more than 350 million items in Amazon's catalogue; therefore, advertising is essential if you want yours to be discovered.

Advantages of utilizing Fulfillment by Amazon (FBA)

The FBA way of doing things is among the best means to develop the business and obtain the products before even more individuals. Amazon has an army of customers that are loyal, which means increased revenue for you.

Several advantages of FBA are listed below:

Management of earnings

Processing return shipping is a pain. From coping with upset customers to inspecting return shipping and controlling the management aspects, Amazon manages all of this for you. They handle customer inquiries, return delivery labeling, and overturn logistics. They do charge a returns processing charge, though it is worthwhile because of the amount of labor they remove from your shoulders.

Customer care management

Amazon has global recognition for giving outstanding customer care. They provide 24/7 assistance via telephone, email, and chat. This eases the customer's minds and also removes an enormous load of work off your plate.

Potentially limitless storage room

Using FBA would mean you do not need to be concerned about just how much or maybe just how small storage room you need for the products. You do not need to purchase a warehouse or be worried about what size of factory you need. There aren't any inventory minimums, which means you can send as small as only one item. Besides, sellers with higher inventory performance scores get limitless storage space from Amazon, so there's that too.

Effortless logistics and delivery

If you have previously handled your very own fulfillment, you understand it could be time-consuming. Higher sales mean more hours spent shipping and packing, or maybe cash invested hiring someone to deal with it. FBA enables you to delegate the whole process, using their experience and expertise.

Discounted delivery rates

Amazon's contracts with the shipping carriers give them good discounts on shipping expenses. They then pass those deals onto sellers in decreased shipping costs when sending the inventory to Amazon. Customers also gain because several orders on Amazon are qualified for free shipping. Also, Prime members receive free two-day shipping on every FBA product - a massive motivator which results in higher income.

Fast delivery

Amazon has plenty of fulfillment centers all around the globe. And so, no matter where your clients are, they can reliably obtain items sent to them within only a few days. When they place an order, Amazon automatically figures out the fulfillment center is nearest to the customer and ships the order from there.

Fulfillment of orders from various other channels.

Amazon's Multi-Channel Fulfillment program makes it possible to market items on various other routes while using Amazon to satisfy those orders. You can also automate the procedure free of charge by utilizing the FBA Shipping app. It instantly sends orders from your shop to Amazon for fulfillment. Additionally, it pulls tracking information and order updates from Amazon, mailing that information to the customers from the store.

What is Private Labeling?

You recognize exactly how in Walmart you can purchase Colgate toothpaste or maybe the less expensive Walmart brand toothpaste? – That's private labeling. What they do is deal with a factory which produces toothpaste and pays them to provide toothpaste with the Walmart brand on it – That is essentially the way it works.

In the case with you and FBA, what you'll be carrying out is considering product opportunities that are good on Amazon, selecting something after which you get a supplier to produce a comparable or even better model with the brand that you'll subsequently promote on Amazon. We usually choose Chinese manufacturers for many reasons, cheaper production costs, proven shipping modes which are dependable as well as easy sourcing of manufacturers and trading via Alibaba.

The Private Label Business Model

In terms of methods to earn money online, this is certainly among the more complicated versions. But when you get your mind around it, it is not terribly difficult. Additionally, it is extremely scalable, though generally there tend to be more inherent risks to be conscious of.

The drawback is the **price** obviously since you will have to invest cash on samples plus inventory upfront. And so, in case you do not have a minimum of $2000 to invest, it may be advisable to save first – even though you can begin a lot smaller, though it is going to take longer to scale). Lastly, just how much you produce is determined by a couple of things.

But don't forget, whenever you see a story of $15,000 in a month, you do not know the entire story behind the success specifically because $15,000 in sales is very different from $15,000 in earnings. To see figures like $15,000 a month, you will most likely have to create a bigger investment that involves much more risk.

Chapter 2

How to Build an Amazon FBA Business from Scratch?

Now that you understand how you can cope with the strategies and what private labeling is, why don't we dive into getting your Amazon seller account and then selecting a winning product to market, and then finally launching the product.

This particular business model has several moving parts and also may seem overwhelming to start with. But we are going to make it as simple as possible.

Here are some of the easy ways to start an Amazon FBA business from scratch:

Create Your Amazon.com Seller Account

It is important to know that where you are based may limit or restrict you from selling in certain regions.

For example, if you are from a certain part in Africa, you can join the US market, but other parts of Africa require you to sell in the UK region.

There are opportunities in all regions, so don't be discouraged from getting started. You will find out which region you can sell in by going onto the Seller Central homepage.

While you can sign up for your seller account later, you should begin with it right now. I advise signing up with a professional account though you can enroll in a free account, which you can upgrade later on. Please be aware that Amazon is constantly changing the interface to provide better experience for users, therefore some of the buttons may have been moved around by the time you read this book.

Here is just how to do that:

Go to Amazon and then go down on the bottom part of the web page and press "Sell on Amazon." You would see a Welcome screen shows up.

Click the "Start Selling" option under "Sell Professionally" on the lower right

of the screen. The Register and start Selling Today account form will show.

Type the name and email address into the respective areas on the registration form's best sign-in information area. Verify the email address and also pick out and verify a password, which is both easy and secure so that you can recall.

Click the "Agreement" option. This is on the bottom right-hand corner of the bottom part Seller Information area of the registration form. Read the understanding and ensure you can abide by its terms.

Type the legal name or even the legitimate name of the business in the Legal Name part of the document. Amazon seems to prefer sellers who owns and are looking to build their brand, therefore I suggest opening the account with your business details where possible. Especially if you are looking to make this a long term sustainable business. Look at the box in the area labeled Amazon Services Business Solutions Agreement: and simply click "Continue."

Pick the title you'd want to be displayed. Enter it within the best Display Name area on the Account Information form, which shows up when you click "Continue." Choose the business name or maybe a title that explains what you sell, like "We sell bags."

Type your address info into the required areas. Put in the phone number within the "Primary Phone" area before you click on the "Continue" button at the bottom part of the form. It is essential to insert your address exactly as it is stated on the proof of address document you submit as supporting documents. I cannot stress how important this is as it will help you avoid lots of back and forth communication with the Amazon team.

Click "Continue" and then choose the credit card type with the drop-down menu at the pinnacle. Type the name (as it is on the card) and your credit card number in the Credit Card Number field. Choose the expiration date of the card as well.

Type your billing street address and telephone info. Do this in the "Enter a Billing Address just for the new Credit Card" area of the form below the part for your card details.

Click the "Continue" button at the bottom part of the display to move forward on the Identity. Again, lets stress that it is important to insert your name and identity information exactly as it is stated on the legal document you are uploading, for example as it is stated on the passport document. Verification by

Telephone displays and then click on the option marked "No, Call Me within the Next Few Minutes at:" and type in the telephone number in which you can be contacted whether you don't wish being contacted using the number you entered in the *address information field*, or exit and leave the default choice in case you do wish to be called using that number.

Click the "Call Me Now" button and note the four-digit PIN in the Call in Progress area.

Type the PIN you are given with the keypad when prompted to do this when Amazon calls.

Click the "Continue" switch and go on to the last screen. Tick the checkbox to show you consent to the conditions of your new Pro Merchant account and simply click the "Confirm" button. You're now prepared to start listing things and marketing with your new Pro Merchant bank account.

If you are from the U.S., you can skip to Part two.

Creating Your Amazon.com Account if you are planning to sell in Amazon's U.K region.

If you are from the U.K., you can simply go on and sign up, making use of the U.K. business details, address, and bank account.

By signing up to sell in the UK market, you will gain entry to the European region which will present further opportunities for expansion later on. You can start marketing on Amazon.co.uk if you feel more comfortable with it, though the product sales volume is reduced on average compared with Amazon.com US market.

For UK-based sellers aiming to promote in the U.S., Europe and the U.K., you must set yourself in place as being a single trader or maybe LLC before you commence registration – you'll have to publish your UTR - unique tax reference number once you sign up with Amazon.

Amazon.co.uk is extremely picky about this type of thing, and the verification process can take some time. They're fast to suspend your account, so keep that in mind. Setting in place as a single trader is painless and quick, most of the information is on the UK GOV site.

Well done, your account is prepared to get sales and, it is time to go into fun things like product research.

Chapter 3

Choosing the Right Product

This section talks about how you can find products to sell on Amazon because this is vital to determining how well you will perform as an Amazon seller.

I am going to show you the golden filters which will provide you a product to market via Private Labelling. Please note that the naturally competitive landscape is changing all the time, so do your own due diligence as well.

Pre-Research Information

Some categories in Amazon are gated, which means you need the authorization to vend there before you can then list products – To avoid spending hours and often days doing product research, you can check out some tools like, Jungle Scout, Egrow, Helium 10, AMZ tracker, Scope, feedback Genius, the list is endless. Jungle Scout and Helium 10 are the highest rated and most recommended tools out there. These tools integrate into your Google Chrome web browser as a web extension, streamlining your product, or service research. It allows you to rank products, check FBA fees, project profitability, see sales volumes, quantity, do vital keyword searches and so much more - without actually leaving the browser or even being forced to get into an Amazon product page.

Many products offer a free trial period, however to get the most from the tools, you will need to sign up to their monthly subscription programs. There are different tiers, catering for different needs, and various price tags with each tier. Be sure to include this in your total start up budget. You should be prepared to fork out at least two months' worth of subscription premiums before the product you land on starts covering the cost of the subscription services.

Do your own research on each of the tools and see which tool you are most comfortable with then decide on the best one using price, usability and so forth into account.

How you can Research Products for Amazon FBA

Here is just how I recommend starting your research. It is essential to monitor everything to be sure of where you are headed.

Create a spreadsheet and record column

This could show item title, number of the same products, top seller rank (BSR), number of reviews. But again, most of the product research tools have the functionality to download the information they have provided in excel. See, most of the groundwork is done to gear you up for success.

Start searching the pinnacle 100 to 500 best sellers in each category.

Because of the growing competition levels, you may wish to do much more than that. To save some time, you can simply get started by viewing and researching products based on the Best Sellers in a product category you are interested in.

It is important to stop yourself from gravitating toward products you are overly passionate about as that will cloud your judgement and cause you to lose time and money in the long run. Focus on what makes sense based on your product research figures and not what you "think will and should sell".

Add items to the spreadsheet

Add items to the spreadsheet which meet criteria's like:

- Small
- Lightweight
- Not sophisticated (be careful of electronic goods)
- Sell for more than twenty dollars

Listed here are a few kinds of stuff you do not wish to do:

- Do not pick dietary supplements or consumables as your very first product.
- Do not select a garlic press, chopping panel, yoga mat, or maybe silicone baking mat – some items are starting to be viciously overpopulated.
- Do not be emotionally connected to the product. Let the figures do the talking.

Repeat the procedure for each category and subcategories on Amazon that interests you.

Other Research Strategies for Finding Products on Amazon

Always use your exclusive experience or knowledge when exploring items, particularly in case you have a specialized niche site.

For instance, as a boxer, Josh may be ready to create several interesting boxing-related items. Or maybe he may be ready to come up with good chances on a current boxing product and also develop a brand around it then use his audience as a launch list. If you have a larger budget and wish to begin with a higher-end device, put it on the table.

I do not advocate electronics due to the likely high defect rate. But in case you truly desire to operate with an electronic device, by all means, get it done if your research proves the figures to be sensible.

The last choice must be made based on a blend of fascination and profit margins. As I stated before – let the figures to do the talking. You should be aiming for a profit margin of at least 30% after FBA, product and shipping is taken into account.

Refining the Short List for Possible Amazon FBA Products

Now we are ready for a deep dive into each item, so for each listed item, perform the following:

Search the primary keyword in Amazon: and check out the leading ten sellers on the first page.

Find Products with Under 500 Reviews: If most of the top 10 have much more than 600 reviews, cross them off the list.

Look for products under 5,000 Best Seller Rate: If the top Seller Rate is more than 5000 for nearly all of the top ten within the primary group, cross it off because your objective is making certain that all of the top 10 are receiving sensible income, if just the one at the top has a great BSR, this will be a slow seller.

The exception happens when your item is much costlier. In that case, you will see fewer units sold each day, therefore creating a greater BSR. Also remember, the BSR is the thing that provides you with a concept of everyday sales volume. By placing probably, the Best Seller Rate into the FBA toolkit, you are going to get an approximate idea of everyday sales volume, but simply make certain you double the estimate provided there as the tool is not correct sometimes.

Note in the spreadsheet the number of products that are similar: The basic objective is finding an item that's selling close to ten pieces daily at more than $20, has under 300 reviews as well as beatable competitors – beatable signifies minimal or not overly high review count, images, bad copy, poor optimization.

To verify estimated sales, type in the very best Seller Rate on FBA Toolkit and double the outcome you see.

To distinguish yourself, you might wish to intentionally begin with a reduced amount of items to stay away from the competition. You will probably find it simpler to market five units each day and release far more products performing five units one day.

A Fast Method to Validate a likely Product for Amazon FBA

The quickest and fastest method to obtain a sense for an item is ordering a small batch from Alliexpress. For $60, you can have a dozen possible units, send them right to Amazon and discover exactly how they do before committing to a larger order. If you're satisfied with those test incomes, you can then discover a dealer for that item and ramp up the purchase volume.

Finding a Supplier on Alibaba

Now, we are planning to discuss the way you locate and choose a supplier.

Sign up on Alibaba – though you can, also, browse local suppliers

Create an account with Alibaba and begin to search for the item you have researched or similar items. You will find a huge selection that could suit your needs.

Search for the supplier

This can be very daunting at first, however like everything in life we fear what we don't understand. With the right knowledge and not overlooking the red flags you will be fine. There is often a sense of danger when managing a new supplier, but here are a few things to support you in finding a good one:

- Only look at the vendors who are verified, has a gold mark (which is debatable, but still useful), which has supplied on Alibaba for a minimum of 3 years and have versatile payments – T/T, escrow, PayPal etc. To locate this supplier, simply make use of the advanced search for Alibaba verified and gold suppliers that offer trade insurance. The most important factor is to ensure your supplier offers trade insurance. This means, all transactions have to be concluded on Alibaba.com and should your supplier not honor the contractual obligations, you can lodge a claim with Alibaba for the purchase value of your shipment.

- Look for FOB and OEM for delivery – OEM means you can use private labelling. FOB indicates freight – essentially, the delivery quote from the factory to your doorstep (FBA warehouse), instead of forking over the expense of shipping goods to port/airport, which is usually expensive.
- Make certain their minimum order quantity (MOQ) is reasonable to you. This is generally in place for negotiation, but getting started, you may not have the funds for, 1000 units, and it is much more of a threat.
- Look for suppliers who manufactures the item that you looking for as well as similar items. They should not be in different types of manufacturing industries as this is a sign that they not the manufacturer and rather a consultant. A Manufacturer would also have an industrial
- address and not an office address. However, some manufacturers do not have trade documentation and would then use a consultant to distribute their goods.
- It is also important to have a look at the annual turnaround and reviews from previous customers in your region.
- Keep in mind that Alibaba is a bidding site and that, occasionally, suppliers will indicate cheaper prices and MOQs to lure you in. Be sure you get the figures checked and negotiate as far as possible. All above information can be obtained on Alibaba and the supplier website.

When you have a small list of suppliers that meet those requirements, it is time to get samples from your shortlist.

Place a Sample Order, Check Quality and get the Full Order

Once you have located a supplier for your chosen product, request a sample which is usually free, however you will still have to pay for shipping to your chosen address.

Something to remember on sample cost

Do not be shocked if the provider bills you $300 for a tiny sample of five units. This is not the provider attempting to trick you. They may have to adjust molds – that is expensive – and maybe, they could be testing to find out if you're serious.

These factories create a huge number of units each month, so they do not have all of the time for a small-time operation, attempting to haggle and make a deal more than $30 to $50.

Take the price as an operation's cost, and you would be looked at as an expert business person. Remember, you are creating a brand name right here, so this is an element of the process. If the sample is great, it is time to place your very first serious order.

If the samples are bad – and this happens sometimes – you will get back on the hunt on Alibaba to locate a new provider. According to the product, the supplier dance can take some time.

Something to remember on paying your supplier

Most vendors won't take PayPal for the key order because of the associated costs.

Options for payment are credit card payment and T/T transfers.

If you truly believe in the supplier, you can utilize T/T, and that is essentially a wire transfer out of your savings account to theirs. Typically speaking, this is probably the riskiest choice, so do this at your discretion.

Always pay on the Alibaba site to ensure trade assurance is available.

Sending the Goods

Air courier mail is largely used for first-time orders, and the suppliers will have the ability to get you great speed. Much bigger orders or even heavier products often get mailed by sea. But commonly, you will reach this point when an item has proven itself, and also, you find out what your product sales are doing. Air freight is more expensive. Whether you are shipping by air, sea or rail (used for shipping from China to European regions), they all have their own pros and cons.

It is a wise decision to make use of prep and shipper initially with new suppliers as sometimes, quality can differ from the samples and so they can easily handhold you through your very first Amazon FBA shipment. Conversely, if you're currently in the U.S. and have chosen a local product supplier, you can simply get the products, identify them yourself, and mail them off to Amazon.

Chapter 4

Keyword Research

This is one thing you can do as you hold out for the product to show up immediately after choosing what products you'd want to sell. The software you have purchased will have an Amazon keyword search functionality.

I have listed a few additional resources for this to help you get started:

- Google keyword planner: It is free and provides you with a great impression of Google's most searched phrases. While not Amazon-specific, you need to include the large volume words into the spreadsheet.
- Uber Suggest: A website that suggests long-tail keyword ideas.
- Keyword Tool Dominator: It is free for three searches each day and also provides you with info on popular key phrases searched in Amazon of the respective Amazons. A good spot to get ideas, particularly for keyword research in some other languages.
- Merchant words: This is a favorite for lots of and costs $30 per month. Nevertheless, it is for the U.S. Amazon just as of this writing.

When you have a good summary of phrases, keep them on file as you will require them for your listing and your PPC campaigns later on.

Adding the Product to Amazon and Creating Your Listing

You will have to put in your listing to Amazon's catalog, it is really easy and here is how:

- From within your seller main account:
- Click Inventory, Add Product, Create A New Product
- Choose the best category for the product.
- Fill out the necessary areas. The fields are going to be different based on the product category.
- Enter your barcode/UPC. This can be purchased on EBay.
- Fill in all you can, such as the keywords and product dimension, and so on.

You will purchase one UPC code for one type of item. Once purchased, you can attach the UPC code to your item listing on Amazon. Insert your item name on the listing as well as completing the various other listing blocks. Be careful if you are a private label seller and have not registered you brand formally. There are tools on Amazon's seller homepage explaining how to do brand registry. Brand registry was introduced to avoid listing hijackers from selling on your listing and you losing control of your listing. As I mentioned before, you can see that Amazon is really geared toward brands who wishes to expand and build brands.

What you should Add to your Core Listing Elements

Title

Your title is something you need to get right first time round. Look at several of your top-selling competitors, find out what they're tried and tested titles are, and use them for inspiration. Be sure to add as many strong keywords based on your research in the title, though do not blindly stuff all of them in!

Images

This can have a significant effect on sales. Your items are the brand. Good quality pictures which determine whether buyers choose your product or that of a competitor.

Below are a few dos and don'ts:

- Ensure the first picture of the listing, is that of your product with a white background.
- Always make use of a minimum of six to eight high-resolution images.
- Always utilize top-quality 3D or professional rendered images.
- Never be enticed to work with your cellphone camera. Even if you consider the quality of your phone camera excellent, it will not be competitive when placed alongside an experienced photographer's picture.

Apart from simple product images, look at the product's context, set the stage, and show it being utilized. Even when marketing an item as basic as a bowl, images of extremely cute babies consuming from the bowl would do better.

Bullet points

The bullet points are the checkmate, so be sure you try using every one of them! Make them snappy and concise and make certain they spotlight your product's primary benefits and advantages. Buyers like reading bullet points which has emoji's, who knew. It is an important marketing tool.

The issue is designed for the purchaser to envision what making use of the item is going to feel like, and knowing the advantages.

Product description

This is where you are going to need to be a bit of imagination. The aim of your explanation is Attention, Desire, Interest, Action. Inside the copy, you need to add a block with the refund policy, whatever it might be. It is vital because it is going to add a level of trust for potential buyers. Additionally, you should not be selling poor quality items that will produce a ton of refunds – done properly; this could be truly successful.

If you are uncertain of your skill to craft content or are not excellent with words, you can typically discover freelancers to undertake the job type on websites such as freelancers, Fiverr, and Upwork.

The Amazon Launch Formula & Building Reviews

This is the launch method that moves your listing from insignificant to producing product sales and jumpstarts the reviews. Having 5-star reviews is important on Amazon for sales!

Amazon has an early reviewer program which grants early birds discounts to your product by exchanging the review for a discounted product.

Setting up Amazon PPC

Now, before we get into how you can establish your PPC campaign, I wish to speak a bit about the dynamics of Amazon PPC and just how it can boost your natural ranking.

This is how it works: Presuming you have correctly researched the keywords, you have to ensure they're contained in the listing and begin running properly structured Amazon PPC campaigns.

Then, *the following happens:*

- Customer adds in a search term by using Amazon's search area.
- Customer clicks on Sponsored Ad.
- The customer buys the item.
- Amazon usually takes note that the item just purchased ought to position for that search term.
- The greater number of product sales through that search term, the greater your product or service ranks for organic search.

That's exactly how you can increase your product rating.

The best way to Structure Your First Campaigns

You can typically run two to three keyword campaigns at a time, based on the item. Here is how you can do it:

Auto campaign: the very first thing to do is put together an automatic plan. Set the daily budget to at least $50 and search for a cost per click (CPC) of a minimum of $0.75.

These are the suggested starting amounts because $50 each day is a fair budget to check out the keywords and see results, and $0.75 is a great quantity for a keyword bid. Your actual cost per click (CPC) may be lower or higher based on the niche. Also remember, the CPC is driven by just how other individuals are bidding on a specific phrase or word, and, like in virtually any auction, the greater number of bidders, the higher the cost. Whenever your CPC bid is sufficient, Amazon features the ad on the first page, and you pay Amazon whenever which sponsored advertisement is clicked. Run the campaign for seven days, pause it, and also make a keyword report. Your objective is seeing which of the suggested keywords are getting you sales. Take note of these keywords and so produce a mechanical keyword campaign.

Create a mechanical campaign: Insert the top-performing keywords from the automobile campaign you ran, maintaining the budget and CPC. Run for five to seven days and also evaluate the results. Take note of the winners, wildly discard the losers.

Create a new physical plan along with other key phrases to test: Operate similar time and budget frames, except in this particular plan, you will wish to run key phrases you've explored and would like to try. Assuming you have set up your listing correctly and also have the appropriate keywords targeted, you need to see your PPC campaigns begin giving you several effective results.

Rinse and Repeat

When your sales are constant and also you hit around the ten sales a day mark, you can contemplate adding a third or second item or product, ideally ones that complement the first product.

Now the business will essentially be on autopilot. Also, you can expand to additional sales platforms while utilizing Amazon FBA to satisfy the orders and also expand your sales empire!

It may seem expensive; however, it is crucial to the success of your product sales.

Chapter 5

Tips and Tactics to Successfully Sell on Amazon FBA

This is a bonus section to give you extra information on how you can successfully make great sales on Amazon FBA.

Research competitors to access lucrative products

Begin by looking at Amazon's best sellers. It is best never to go to the top sellers as a beginner, though you can buy a concept of what types of items are widely used. Plug those things into a program such as Jungle Scout, Egrow or Helium 10. These tools provide all sorts of juicy information like estimated monthly

income, keyword searches competitor intel & fee calculators.

Be sensible about what items you sell.

Constantly check out product sales ranking. High ranking products sell fast, but there is a great deal more competition. Low ranking and even non-existent solutions could be slow sellers, which lead to long-term storage fees. But since there is very little to no competition, it is less complicated to be the predominant seller for all those listings. Once you understand the product sales rank, you will be aware of what you are up against.

Start small

You do not need to have a huge selection of items to start your own online business. Discover the ropes with just a couple of solutions at first. It is easier to produce an organized, seamless process when you simply have a small number of things. After the procedure is in place, it is less complicated to scale up and also increase the items as you develop.

Build a brand

When you would like to stick out from the ocean of Amazon sellers, you will require your own brand, which means having full knowledge of the target buyers, learning how to place the brand, and developing constantly styled product pictures, descriptions and titles. Creating your very own web shop in which you manage the consumer experience to enhance Amazon product sales will be the simplest way to accomplish this.

You can additionally utilize special presentations and inserts to ensure your brand personality sticks out upon delivery. Packaging, which encourages buyers to register for the email list or perhaps following social profiles, is also a great starting place.

Use great SEO practices

Amazon is a really competitive industry; therefore, it could be hard to get your products discovered. Like Google, Amazon is the search engine with ranking factors that decide what items to show for any product search. You can get much higher in the search engine results by exploring what keywords folks use when looking for the products and utilizing those keywords throughout your product or service listings.

Get great product photos

Amazon calls for the primary product image to show just the item against a white-colored background. Because your pictures are a customer's very first impression of the products, ensure they're ideal. Don't forget, buyers cannot touch the products when you are marketing on the internet; therefore, you want the photos to be as attractive as possible.

Display the item from various perspectives, display it in motion, show close-ups of different functions, and clearly show an individual carrying it. Consider getting 360-degree videos and images produced to generate merchandise pages that much more engaging.

Optimize your product or service titles

Ever notice just how a great deal of Amazon products has long, detailed titles? That is sellers attempting to stuff the keywords in. Amazon allows up to 250 figures for titles, but that does not mean it is wise to make use of all 250 characters. In reality, Amazon is noted to control product listings with excessively lengthy titles. And so, the objective is always to be descriptive and also to the stage while continually obtaining your primary keyword into the name. It provides crucial info without going crazy.

Optimize the bullet points

As I stated before, when a buyer clicks through to the product, among the very first things they are searching for are the bullet points. If those bullets do not respond to the questions or even possess the specifics they need to have, they are more likely to move to a competitors listing. And so, be sure to offer clients all of the info needed to create a purchase decision. Address common issues, concentrate on your product's advantages, and also include significant product details. The same as with the title, you need to add those keywords in without going crazy.

Develop a thorough item description

Provide extensive directions, increase the product photographs, toss in several short videos, and add your brand story. Customers want to know precisely what they are receiving and who they are getting it from whenever they purchase the product.

Answer questions

One of Amazon's distinctive features will be the question and answer section. Virtually anyone can submit a question about a product, whether it has been bought by them or perhaps not, and people can submit a solution, whether they have bought the item or perhaps not. Many sellers believe they have to hold out for buyers to ask questions. Though you can boost engagement by getting started yourself. Ask a buddy to submit a question that is generally asked about the product. After that, you publish the answer, along with this, clients discover you are a helpful and involved seller.

Get Good Reviews

It has been proven time and time again that individuals are much more prone to purchase items when they have positive reviews. When individuals are uncertain about anything, they shop around to find out what other folks are performing or even thinking. If many buyers say Product X is wonderful, so no one says something about Product Y, guess what type buyers will purchase?

Pick the best repricing program

Prices change consistently on Amazon, and although probably the lowest price does not constantly gain the purchase package, it usually does. Many Amazon sellers employ repricing software to change the prices throughout the day immediately

Use Amazon Marketing Services (AMS)

AMS is an advertising tool enables you to produce advertisements for the products and focus on them based on similar products or keywords. Additionally, it offers performance analytics so that you can optimize the ads.

Frequent Asked Questions

Will I place all the merchandise in all of the groups on Amazon?

Preceding authorization could be expected to list certain goods in certain categories.

Precisely why must I sell on Amazon?

Amazon is the leading market for selling goods globally. You are placing your product in front of millions of Amazon customers which means a larger buyer audience, and therefore higher sales possibilities. All without creating and maintaining your own e-commerce website.

What is offered on Amazon?

This program permits businesses and individuals to market their inventory and products on the Amazon platform.

What types of items can't be listed on Amazon?

Some items might not be added in summary for factors of compliance with regulatory limitations like prescription medications or pictures of crime scenes.

Does Amazon protect against fraud?

Yes. Amazon Payment Fraud Protection allows you to eradicate fraudulent orders on products.

What is the best way to open a new Amazon merchant account?

You may sign up for the seller account of the choice, without needing to contact a seller by clicking on the Sell as

Professional or maybe Sell as Individual buttons on the Amazon page.

Before registering, access the following info:

- An international billing charge card with a legal billing address
- A phone number for the procedure of registration
- your tax identity info
- Business name, contact information, and address.

Can I stop my pro sales account?

Sellers can change at any time to a private product sales plan by modifying their account settings. Your account remains open, plus you can continue sending things to Amazon as a private seller. You won't have a chance to access the advantages of the business account, like bulk load orders and reports, shipping prices customized by the provider and listing functions.

Just how can I shut down my Amazon merchant bank account?

For individuals that wish to shut down the account completely, vendor support can help. Remember, you can utilize the ad status feature to prevent the ads. You can additionally eliminate the ads while keeping the account for later use. Before closing the account, stop and also delete the lists and solve most transactions.

Do Amazon sellers earn money?

Millions of small businesses and medium worldwide use Amazon for product sales. The vast majority of products purchased in Amazon stores are available from these companies. Typically, medium and small businesses based in the USA. have sold over $100,000 at Amazon stores.

Just how can I generate revenue in U.S., Canadian and Mexican markets?

When you start as an experienced seller, you will be eligible to make revenue in Amazon marketplaces in Canada, Mexico, and the U.S. by way of a consolidated North American bank account. This can allow it to be simpler for you to talk about product listing info and control your inventory regularly in all three markets. For those transaction costs per product, sellers will spend the costs associated looking where the item was sold. If perhaps you're a professional seller, one monthly subscription would be billed for the sale in North America.

When you're currently selling to Amazon in Canada, or Mexico, United States, you can utilize your present account to get payments inside your local currency

with the Amazon Currency Converter. In case you're a new seller who desires to promote in the United States, Canada, or Mexico, you'll be able to be paid right to the local bank account in regional currency, ideal if Amazon has billed your local account.

What's the price of selling on Amazon?

Two sales plans are featured by amazon. At the time of writing this book, the professional sales program can be obtained for a monthly membership fee of roughly $40 and a product sales charge per item, that differs by group.

When you intend to market under fifty products per month, individual plans might be much better. There's no payment amount rate; rather, individuals pay $0.99 per product sold and additional marketing costs, that differ by category.

What's the cost of beginning Amazon FBA?

Amazon's processing expenses vary significantly based on numerous factors, like the size and the mass of the products you're promoting. The expense of applying FBA for the merchandise is estimated by visiting the FBA webpage for rates.

At what time do I get labeled the monthly charge for membership?

Amazon's monthly billing payment applies just to pro sales accounts and starts once you complete the registration method. The first monthly subscription would be charged then except stated otherwise in advertising offers.

How can you handle my merchant account?

You can use the Seller Central site to tackle all aspects of selling on Amazon. This is the website where you tackle everything related to your seller account, bring product info, update list, handle orders, and handle payments.

What is the best way to add to your inventory?

You have four choices to post product data:

- Use Excel listing documents to create numerous products concurrently.
- Use the Amazon Marketplace web program to publish and receive reports in bulk.
- Use the Add Product function in Seller Central to write a single item at the same time.
- Use the Sell on Amazon key element on Amazon product sites.

How can I understand a sale is made?

Amazon tells you by email or SMS when you get an order. You can pick one of the notification techniques in your account settings.

Exactly how much is the charge to deliver items that I sell?

If you place your orders yourself, Amazon delivery costs apply to multimedia products offered by sellers. Shipping costs are charged based on the product category and shipping system selected by the customer, after which transfer the amount. For items that Amazon provides for you and the Amazon Sell fees, charges will be billed for order fulfillment, storage space, and suggested services.

Just how does Fulfillment by Amazon work?

With Fulfillment by Amazon, you keep the goods at Amazon distribution facilities. We choose, pack, ship, and also afford customer service for these items.

What's referred to as the buy Box?

Amazon Buy Box is the chart holding a product information page where customers begin the investment procedure by inputting things to the baskets. A crucial facet of the Amazon platform is the fact that comparable products have many suppliers. If some vendors offer the related product in a "new" state, they'll contest for the package of this item.

To compete with the Buy Box positioning, sellers should demonstrate that they continually produce a great shopping experience for customers. Performance-based criteria are used by us to find out the eligibility and also the condition of the placement. Eligible Buy Box ads that don't gain the Buy Box are qualified to be positioned in the More Box Purchase agreements. Amazon doesn't ensure the appointment in just about any of these places.

What is Fulfillment by Amazon (FBA)?

This is a program on Amazon which enables you to keep your merchandise in the Amazon warehouse. Amazon packs and provide orders to customers, provide customer service, and also handle returns.

What exactly are the advantages of Amazon's conformity (FBA)?

When your items are listed through Fulfillment by Amazon, they are going to be qualified for the following operates on Amazon.

Expand the business and also utilize Amazon's recognized order management technologies.

Pleasure the clients with world-class customer service to process the orders.

No development problems: FBA can help vendors adjust their functions flexibly and with no new investments in labor and warehouses. Amazon can withstand a broad range of huge volumes and product types.

In what groups can I work with FBA?

You can offer things in the following groups: Baby items, gear, kitchen, Jewelry, movies, mobile phones, video games, toys, tablets, personal CPUs, Home appliances, Digital accessories, Consumer electronics, Books, Beauty, as well as wristwatches. Additional groups are still to come.

Do I need a summary of the least number of products?

FBA doesn't keep the least number of items to make use of it.

Just how can I take part in the FBA system?

You can take part in FBA through your contact info when using the Contact Us link. Amazon is going to reply after reviewing the info in the next steps. When approved, you have to register on the Amazon distribution facility as an extra site of business with the tax establishments.

Can I purchase Amazon as an additional institution?

Yes. When you have been accepted into the Amazon plan, you should register the Amazon distribution facility as an extra site of business with the tax authorities. Nevertheless, in case you sell just VAT excused books, which might

not be essential. Please note that if you begin selling items subject to fees under Amazon plan, you have to register following the Sales Tax Law by adding our distribution facility as an extra site of business with the tax authorities.

Do I have to market on Amazon to make use of FBA?

Yes. FBA is only accessible to sellers who sell on Amazon.

How about the picture of my brand?

Orders performed by Amazon are delivered in boxes of the Amazon brand. The delivery notes, as well as the invoice, reveal the name as being a merchandise seller.

What exactly are the FBA rates?

The following services are in the FBA rate:

- Collect and also package the products when requested by a customer.
- Keep the products in the Amazon Distribution Center.
- Increase the coverage of the products on Amazon.
- Shipment of your items to the customer.

- Customer service and also returns appropriately with Amazon for items offered on Amazon.

Exactly how will I be charged Amazon Fulfillment?

Amazon will subtract the FBA charge of the approved item to your Amazon Seller account and remember the costs Payment of funds.

Do you use the weight or minimum weight of merchandise to be shipped by the FBA?

The actual weight of 500 grams is utilized by amazon compliance.

Just how can I download the ads on Amazon?

There are three routes featured by FBA to obtain your advertisements depending on the dimensions of the business.

Include a product: If you want Amazon to complete a few products, you can

list them one after the other. Seller Central, provider web user interface, help you choose items from the Amazon catalog or even add new ones. When your posts are listed, you can just turn them to Amazon files.

Flat file flows: If you have a large number of elements, you can list them by downloading a flat-file through our web application. Amazon presents an Excel spreadsheet template you can make use of to produce the file. This process enables you to list them immediately for Amazon compliance.

API Integration: If you have a lot of expansion elements and materials, you can incorporate your website or maybe an inventory control program into the Amazon inventory catalog.

This process enables you to list them immediately for delivery by Amazon.

Just how can I carry the items for shipment?

Retrieve your packaged and also labeled products and carry them in containers to post on the Amazon Distribution Center. For your packages, ensure you are printing labels for shipments. You can print the merchandise list out of your seller account and also amounts that you would like to send to Amazon and also utilize the list as being a guide when collecting items from the store.

Congest your devices using several containers as you can. Be sure you protect items during delivery damage with the addition of softening material, such as bubble wrap on the package. Check the taped-up package to ensure that the items in the box don't shift during delivery and that the package is resilient enough to be delivered. Repack the package if necessary.

The best way to prepare the products which are delivered to you?

Every product you deliver to Amazon should be prepared, packed, and also delivered to customers. Fragile products must be individually wrapped with a defensive substance like polystyrene foam or maybe bubble wrap.

Must I tag my product?

Each device has to be marked; therefore, the appropriate merchandise is selected from the Amazon distribution facility inventory and delivered to the client. Labels also help monitor the devices you've in listing at Amazon distribution facilities. Shipments gotten with no appropriate labeling could be offered too.

You can print labels within your merchant account.

What units need labeling?

Each device has to be labeled working with or perhaps not with the labels offered by its supplier.

Will Amazon compensate for misplaced or even damaged units?

In case of damage to a product in situations where Amazon presumes accountability under the Amazon Services Agreement, Amazon will refund you.

How is consumer reimbursement handled?

We need to accept consumer refunds for products or services returns for items sold through the Amazon site in conformity with Amazon's return policy, conditions, and FBA terms. Such refunds will be revealed in your Amazon sales report.

What is Amazon Prime?

Amazon Prime is a loyalty program that offers complimentary one-day and two-day delivery of a huge selection of a huge number of qualifying items to Amazon customers in over a hundred nations. Amazon Premium users will take advantage of reduced rates on the thousands of products sent on time, on the very same day and early in the day in the twenty cities. Prime members have access that is easy to the greatest Lightning deals, and also exclusive covets offers.

Just how can I get into the Amazon Prime program?

All Amazon items sold at Amazon (FBA) are supplied with prime services. As an FBA merchant, all of these products are Premium eligible, and additionally, the Premium Badge is found on Amazon. On that foundation, the customers are going to enjoy a no-cost, limitless one day and two days delivery of the goods in over a hundred cities.

www.ingramcontent.com/pod-product-compliance
Lightning Source LLC
Chambersburg PA
CBHW030535220526
45463CB00007B/2844